I Go With God

Written by Jill Ferrie
Illustrated by Muhammad Khaidir Syaféi
Designed by Nicolás Pacheco

FERRIETALES PUBLISHING, LLC
Cresco Iowa

I Go With God

No part of this publication may be reproduced in whole or in part or stored in a retrieval system or transmitted in any form or by any means, electronic, mechanical, photocopy, recording, or otherwise, without written permission of the publisher.

Quote by Mary Baker Eddy used courtesy of the Mary Baker Eddy Collection.

For information regarding permission write to FerrieTales, 3690-318th Ave., Cresco, Iowa 52136

ISBN 978-0-9976560-0-8

Text and illustrations copyright © 2018 by FerrieTales Publishing
All rights reserved
Published by FerrieTales Publishing

Visit us at www.igowithgod.com

I Go With God
written by Jill Ferrie
illustrated by Muhammad Khaidir Syaféi
designed by Nicolás Pacheco

Dear reader,

I Go With God builds on the spiritual healing truth that "God is our refuge and strength, a very present help in trouble" (Psalms 46:1) as discovered by everyday people in our favorite Bible stories. In this story a young boy shows us that God's power is as present for us today as it was years ago. He also helps us understand that:

- God is Spirit and, therefore, He is ever-present.

- Prayer helps us feel God's presence and love.

- Angels are God's way of helping us.

Angels are defined as "God's thoughts passing to man;..." in the Christian Science textbook, *Science and Health with Key to the Scriptures* by Mary Baker Eddy (p. 581). As such, when we pray, we can all hear His healing thoughts in our time of need.

As the young boy in this story learns, "Listening to God is a good way to pray. His angels chase all those bad feelings away."

I jumped out of bed and started my day.
I said hi to Puffer my usual way.

"Hey friend!"

Puffer's my goldfish,
he swims in a bowl.
I feed him by nine,
at least that's my goal.

But something was wrong,
I felt really bad.
I wasn't myself,
I got very sad.

I needed help fast,
I had a big day.
My friend's birthday party
was hours away.

But I wasn't up for doing that job.

I wanted to lie on that bed like a blob.

Then I remembered
the best help that I knew,
our Father in heaven,
God -- you know Him too.

God is Spirit,
He fills every spot.
In fact, there's no place
where His power is not.

So I prayed to God like I know how to do. When I pray I get quiet. What do you do?

Good thoughts filled my mind—
they floated right in.

Good thoughts are angels.
I started to grin.

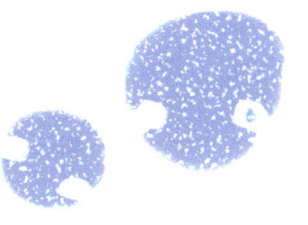

God gives us those angels,
they're easy to hear-

right when we need them,
they're helpful and clear...

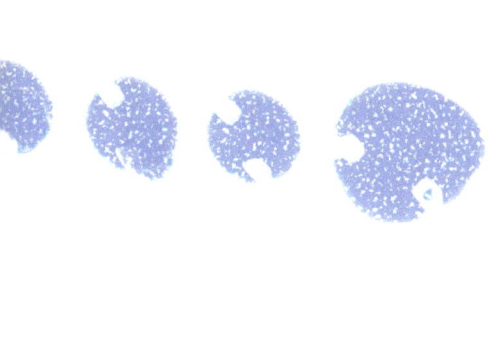

like paying attention
when crossing the street
so cars passing by
don't run over our feet.

Angels kept coming and filling my mind.

My thoughts were all happy and loving and kind...

like hugging a friend
to show her I care,

and laughing so hard
that I fall off my chair,

and singing and dancing
and helping my neighbor

find her lost cat
named Rusty Van Sleighbor.

I suddenly noticed
I felt so much better.
I jumped up from my bed
and put on my red sweater.

Like the air that I breathe but don't ever see, the **power of prayer** is always with me.

Listening to God is a good way to pray.
His angels chase all those bad feelings away.

So when you need help, just ask God, it's all cool. He's everywhere you are, even at school.

I made my bed quickly and picked up my toys.

I ran to my Puffer, he made a strange noise.

He felt it! He got it!
It was easy to see

that God helped my Puffer
just like He helped me.

And so it was time to be on my way. I left for the party, ready to play.

Wherever I go,
whatever I do,
I go with God.
You go with Him too!

Can you get Puffer to his bowl?

For more activities visit www.igowithgod.com

www.ingramcontent.com/pod-product-compliance
Lightning Source LLC
Chambersburg PA
CBHW041538040426
42446CB00002B/147